ISBN - 978-0-9917887-6-7

This book is dedicated to my beloved parents Elizabeth and Thomas.

Special thanks to Angel Brkic whose artistic talents brought these words to life.
I am so grateful for the love and support of my dear husband Barry and all my family and friends that encouraged me along the way.

Matlox publishing

Lizzy, Victoria, and Tommy were walking home from school and talking about Liam, a boy in their class who said and did mean things to a lot of the kids.

Tommy said, "He really does pick on Suzy a lot." Just as Tommy said that, Suzy ran by them crying, while Liam chased her all the way to her house.

Victoria said, "Liam does bully us a lot of the time, but do you notice how unhappy he looks? Let's think of some way we can help him so he doesn't want to bully anyone anymore.

That evening after Lizzy had finished supper, her friend Suzy called. She was crying and said that she did not want to go back to school because Liam was so mean to her and she was afraid of him.

Lizzy tried to comfort Suzy the best she could.

Lizzy sat on her bed and thought about what she could do to help Suzy.

The next day at school Lizzy told Tommy and Victoria that she had an idea that could stop Liam from bullying. Both Tommy and Victoria agreed that it was a great idea.

Lizzy spoke to the teacher about her plan and the teacher loved it.

Lizzy stood up and said, "I want to do three nice things for someone and then I will choose another friend to do three nice things for someone else and then they choose a friend to do three nice things until everyone in the class has done three nice things for someone else.
That way we can show kindness every day."

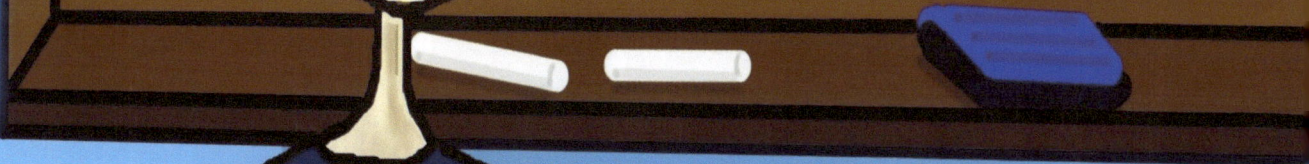

When Lizzy finished explaining her kindness plan, Liam yelled "that is so dumb, just like you Lizzy" and then he laughed and shook his head.

Well, Liam Lizzy said, "You are the first friend I want to choose to do three kind things for someone today."

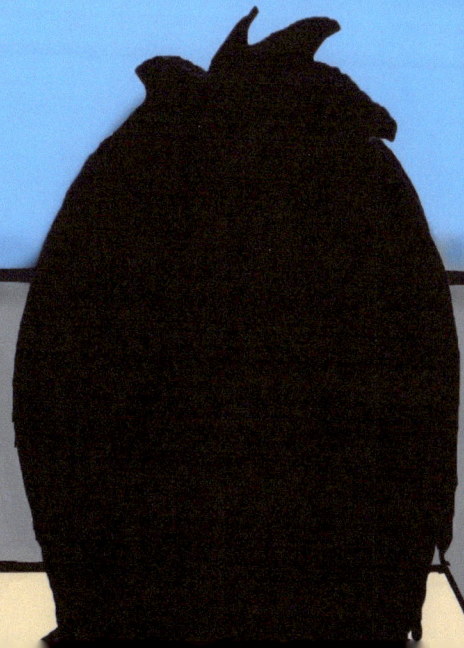

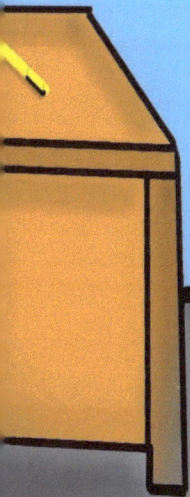

Liam looked surprised as he said, "I can't believe that you called me your friend and you chose me first."

"Yes" said Lizzy."I know you will be very good at this because you have a kind heart." Liam smiled and said "thank you. I will do it."

Liam looked around the room and said "the first thing I will do is to say I am sorry for all the mean things I have said and done to all of you. Will you forgive me?"

The class looked around as a chorus of "yes we forgive you Liam" rang out. Then Liam turned and said "thank you Lizzy for calling me your friend and for choosing me first.

No one has ever done that before and I did not think anybody liked me."

The next thing Liam did was to give all the kids in the class a hug. When he saw Suzy he said "I really like you Suzy and I want to be your friend." Suzy smiled and said, "I would like that."

Then the teacher said "Thank you Lizzy that was a wonderful idea. There are so many things we can do to show kindness to others every day. Always remember that kind words or a smile can change people even bullies."

www.ingramcontent.com/pod-product-compliance
Lightning Source LLC
Chambersburg PA
CBHW040628070426
42447CB00039B/154